DOGS

HOUNDS

scent hounds:
  basset
  beagle
  bloodhound
  dachshund
sight or gaze hounds:
  Afghan
  borzoi
  greyhound
  saluki

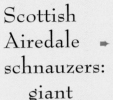

SPORTING DOGS

pointers
retrievers:
  golden
  Labrador
setters
spaniels:
  clumber
  cocker
  English springer
  field
  Welsh springer

TERRIERS

Scottish fox
Scottish
Airedale
schnauzers:
  giant
  standard
  miniature

WORKING DOGS

- Akita
- boxer
- Doberman pinscher
- German shepherd
- Great Dane
- husky
- malamute
- mastiff
- Newfoundland
- rottweiler
- St. Bernard

HERDING DOGS

- American shepherd (U.S.)
- Border collie
- collie (Scotland)
- corgi (Wales)
- Old English sheepdog (England)
- puli (Hungary)
- Shetland sheepdog (Scotland)

These are just a few examples of hounds, sporting dogs, terriers, and working and herding dogs.

SEYMOUR SIMON

DOGS

SCHOLASTIC INC.

New York Toronto London Auckland Sydney
Mexico City New Delhi Hong Kong Buenos Aires

Photo credits: front endpapers, left page: (top left) © 2001 Lynn M. Stone, (top right) © 1998 Ron Kimball / Ron Kimball Photography, Inc., (center left) © 1993 Ron Kimball / Ron Kimball Photography, Inc., (center) © 1999 Ron Kimball / Ron Kimball Photography, Inc., (center right) © 2001 Lynn M. Stone, (bottom right) © 1996 Ron Kimball / Ron Kimball Photography, Inc.; front endpapers, right page: (top left) © 1996 Lynn M. Stone, (top right) © Eunice Pearcy / Animals Animals, (center right) © 1994 Ron Kimball / Ron Kimball Photography, Inc., (bottom left) by Earl W. Hindman, (bottom right) © Tim Davis / Photo Researchers; p. 4 © Ulrike Schanz / Animals Animals; p. 6 © 1997 Ron Kimball / Ron Kimball Photography, Inc.; p. 7 © Lynn D. Odell / Animals Animals; p. 8 © Renee Lynn / Photo Researchers; p. 11 © Robert Maier / Animals Animals; p. 12 © Carol J. Kaelson / Animals Animals; p. 13 © Lynn D. Odell / Animals Animals; p. 15 © Robert Maier / Animals Animals; p. 16 © Carol J. Kaelson / Animals Animals; p. 17 © M. Miller; p. 18 © M. Miller; p. 19 © Henry Ausloos / Animals Animals; p. 20 © 2002 Lynn M. Stone; p. 21 © Robert Dowling / Corbis; p. 22 © 2002 Lynn M. Stone; p. 23 © Gerard Lacz / Animals Animals; p. 24 © 1992 Ron Kimball / Ron Kimball Photography, Inc.; p 25 © Ralph Reinhold / Animals Animals; p. 26 © 1999 Ron Kimball / Ron Kimball Photography, Inc.; p. 27 © Hugh Rose / Visuals Unlimited; p. 28: (top left) © 1988 Ron Kimball / Ron Kimball Photography, Inc., (top right) © 1994 Ron Kimball / Ron Kimball Photography, Inc., (bottom left) © 1990 Ron Kimball / Ron Kimball Photography, Inc., (bottom right) © 1996 Ron Kimball / Ron Kimball Photography, Inc.; p. 30 © 2000 Ron Kimball / Ron Kimball Photography, Inc.; p. 31 © 1999 Ron Kimball / Ron Kimball Photography, Inc.; p. 32: © Tim Davis / Photo Researchers; p. 33 by Meghan Dietsche; p. 34 © J. & P. Wegner / Animals Animals; p. 35 © Gerard Lacz / Animals Animals; p. 36 © Ralph Reinhold / Animals Animals; p. 37 © M. Miller; back endpapers, left page: (top left) © 1988 Ron Kimball / Ron Kimball Photography, Inc., (top right) © 2000 Ron Kimball / Ron Kimball Photography, Inc., (bottom left) © 2001 Lynn M. Stone, (bottom right) © 1987 Ron Kimball / Ron Kimball Photography, Inc.; back endpapers, right page: (top left) © 2000 Ron Kimball / Ron Kimball Photography, Inc., (top right) © Ralph Reinhold / Animals Animals, (bottom left) © William D. Bachman / Photo Researchers, (bottom right) by Alicia Mikles.

To the memory of my dog Nova,
and to my son Mike's dogs,
Reilly and Dizzy

Special thanks to Dan Wharton, Director, Central Park Zoo,
Wildlife Conservation Society, for his expert advice.

The domestic dog is the most popular pet in the world. Tens of millions of dogs live with people as pets, working dogs, or guard dogs.

People and dogs have been together for thousands of years. We have shared shelter and food. We have hunted together, played together, and worked together.

Scientists believe that dogs developed from wolves that had learned to live close to people. Eventually, five breeds of dogs emerged: huge guard mastiffs, wolflike dogs, sheep-herding dogs, greyhounds, and pointer dogs used for hunting. Today there are more than four hundred breeds. Despite their differences, all dogs, from the tiny Chihuahua to the Great Dane, belong to the species *Canis familiaris*.

Many dogs are fast and can run long distances. Some racing dogs, such as the greyhound, can run over forty miles per hour. The fastest human distance runner can run only fifteen miles per hour.

Large domestic dogs have powerful, graceful bodies. Using their strong hind legs, some dogs can jump over a fence several times their own height.

Dogs have strong teeth and jaws that are good for tearing meat. A big dog can bite ten times harder than a person can. Dogs are able to swallow much larger hunks of food than humans are able to swallow. Dogs eat almost anything. A pet dog will eat meat or table scraps or dog chow made partly from grains.

Dogs have five senses, just as we do. But dogs are much more sensitive than we are. A dog can identify a friend from a stranger just by sniffing. You have five million smell cells in your nose. A German shepherd or a bloodhound has more than two hundred million smell cells in its nose. A bloodhound can follow an animal's or a person's odor trail hours after it has been made.

A dog can hear noises that are four times farther away than the noises you can hear. That's why a watchdog barks before you hear any noise. A dog can hear a dog whistle easily. You can barely hear it.

Dogs' eyes are very sensitive to movement. If you stand still, a dog may not notice you. But an insect that moves in the grass will attract its attention. Dogs see mostly gray tones, but they can see some colors, such as the color red.

Dogs are very intelligent, and they learn quickly. A dog instinctively knows how to get along with other dogs. In a pack, dogs have ranks. The leader is the dominant dog, or boss. The others are submissive dogs or followers. Pet dogs usually behave toward their human owner the same way that they would behave toward the boss dog.

When dogs meet, they sniff each other. Sniffing lets a dog know all about another dog: its age, gender (male or female), and rank. When a boss dog meets a follower dog, it shows dominance by raising its head, ears, and tail. A follower dog shows submission by crouching down or rolling over on its back.

Dogs don't use words the way people do. Dogs use different sounds—from angry growling to happy barking to upset whimpering—to express their feelings. Learning "dog talk" will help you understand whether your pet dog is hungry or wants to go out for a walk.

Female dogs usually can have babies by the time they are one year old. After mating with a male dog, a female dog gives birth to a litter of puppies about nine weeks later. Small dogs have litters of about four puppies. Large dogs can have eight or more puppies in their litters.

A mother dog seems to know exactly what to do when her puppies are born. She bites through the umbilical cord that attaches each puppy to her. Then she licks the puppy. Now it can breathe and start suckling. It takes less than two hours for each puppy to be born.

Puppies are born both blind and deaf. For its first week, the puppy just suckles and sleeps. At two weeks, its eyes open. At three weeks, it can move around, focus its eyes, and hear sounds.

At four weeks, the puppy starts playing with its littermates. When you pick up your puppy, it wiggles. It may squeak. The puppy is tiny, but you can feel its muscles moving. Its skin feels warm and dry.

At five to six weeks, the puppy has all its first teeth (milk teeth). It is ready to eat puppy meal or cereal with milk. Between six and ten weeks, the puppy begins exploring its surroundings. It should stay with its mother until it is at least eight to ten weeks old. By then the puppy has stopped nursing.

Of all the dog breeds, hounds may have had the longest ties with people. Hounds were the earliest hunting dogs. People bred them to hunt by sight or smell. Sight or gaze hounds, such as the greyhound and saluki, can use their keen eyesight to spot game from a long distance. Long-legged hounds are also great runners and can run down swift animals.

Scent hounds like the dachshund and bloodhound track prey by smelling the ground for their odors. Scent hounds usually have short, strong legs, long heads with big, floppy earflaps, and big noses. Their sense of smell is as much as one million times better than your sense of smell.

Many modern breeds of hounds are no longer used as hunters. They are kept as pets. Some hounds, such as beagles and bassets, tend to roam. To keep them at home, you need a lot of space and good fences.

Sporting dogs usually have keen senses of smell and sight. Different breeds of sporting dogs range in size from small spaniels to large setters, pointers, and retrievers.

Spaniels are intelligent, small to medium-sized dogs that make excellent pets. They have long noses, and like scent hounds, they have big, floppy earflaps. Spaniels locate and retrieve, and they are also used to flush birds from their hiding places in tall grass. Different kinds of spaniels do different things.

When they spot game, pointers and setters direct their muzzles toward the hunted animal. They are trained to "set," or stand still, for as long as an hour.

Retrievers are strong dogs that locate and bring back game. They are usually good swimmers. Most retrievers, such as the golden and Labrador, make very fine pets because they can be trained easily.

Terriers are small, lively dogs that were first bred in the British Isles. They were used to hunt burrowing animals such as rabbits, foxes, and rats. Terriers were so popular that many European artists painted them. They were also mascots in British military units. Some terriers even won medals for their service in the British army.

Terriers are bouncy, friendly dogs that bark a lot. Because they always seem ready to play, these short-legged, stocky dogs make good pets.

Specially trained breeds of working and herding dogs help people all over the world. German shepherds and sheepdogs herd sheep and cattle. Malamutes and huskies pull sleds across the snow in Alaska. Doberman pinschers and rottweilers act as watchdogs. St. Bernards can locate people lost in the snow.

Guide dogs help visually impaired people find their way. Bloodhounds assist the police by sniffing for drugs or bombs in cars or at airports.

For centuries, farmers and herdsman have used dogs to help guard and move their flocks. Many countries have their own breed of herding dog. In the United States, the Border collie is a common herding dog.

a mixed-breed collie

Nonsporting dogs are as different from one another as you can imagine. They range from the friendly dalmatian with its white coat and black spots to the deeply wrinkled shar-pei, or Chinese fighting dog. The chow chow has a blue-black mouth and tongue. The bichon frise is a fluffy white dog. The bulldog looks tough but has a gentle manner. Still another is the Lhasa apso, a watchdog and a symbol of good fortune in Tibetan temples.

Poodles are one of the most popular nonsporting dogs. They are intelligent, good-natured, friendly, and very loyal—just what people look for in a pet. Because their curly hair doesn't shed but keeps growing, poodles have to be clipped regularly. Poodles vary in size. Standard poodles weigh as much as seventy pounds. Miniature and toy poodles can weigh less than ten pounds.

Toy dogs are kept mostly as lap dogs and pets. The English toy spaniel is a mini version of a full-sized dog. Other toy dogs, such as the Chihuahua and the snub-nosed pug, don't resemble any large dogs.

Four thousand years ago, the Chinese kept "lion dogs" that looked like the Pekingese dogs we have today. Maltese dogs have been found in Egyptian tombs and have been depicted in early Roman paintings. The royal families of England, France, and Russia often included their pet toy dogs in paintings.

Some toy dogs were bred to perform specific jobs. During the Middle Ages, nobles who lived in cold castles and stone buildings sometimes used toy dogs to warm their feet. The Tibetan spaniel could turn prayer wheels. The tiny turnspit was trained to run on a wheel attached to a spit. As the spit turned, the game on the spit was roasted over a fire.

Mixed-breed dogs, or mutts, are all kinds of shapes, colors, and sizes. Sometimes mutts are even friendlier and better tempered than purebreds. They may also adapt more easily to different surroundings.

A mutt is a very special dog. No other dog is exactly like it. When you adopt a mutt as a puppy, you usually don't know who its parents or grandparents are. Sometimes you can tell how big a mutt will become by the size of its paws.

Dogs have different personalities and behaviors. The way a dog is raised and trained also affects its personality and behavior. A dog doesn't have to be purebred to make a wonderful pet.

There are many ways you can get a pet dog. A dog owner you know may offer you a puppy from a new litter. If you adopt a dog from a local animal shelter, make sure the animals there look healthy and well cared for, and ask about the dog you wish to adopt. The dogs are usually given away for free or for a small donation to the shelter.

If you want to buy a purebred dog, ask a pet owner or someone at a local kennel club to recommend a good breeder. Breed rescue clubs sometimes provide foster homes to purebreds that have been abandoned or given away.

Apuppy needs someone to care for it: to feed it, train it, walk it, and pet it. A person needs to spend a lot of time building a good relationship with a puppy. You should get a puppy only if you or someone in your family can do all those things.

Dogs need a great deal of attention and care, too. They have to be fed, groomed, walked, and trained. Some dogs need lots of room. Some dogs can live in small apartments. It's up to you and your parents to decide whether you have the time to care for a dog and whether you have the room for it.

If you do decide to adopt a dog, you will have more than a pet. You will have a lifelong loyal friend and companion.

SO MANY DIFFERENT KINDS OF DOGS

bichon frise

bulldog

◄ chow chow

dalmatian

Lhasa apso ►

poodles:

   standard

 ◄ miniature

   toy

shar-pei (Chinese fighting dog) ►

SO MANY DIFFERENT KINDS OF DOGS

toy dogs:

 Chihuahua

 English toy spaniel

 papillon

 ← Pomeranian

 shih tzu →

 Tibetan spaniel

 turnspit

 Yorkshire terrier

← mixed breeds →